The Expressive

BY

Kristopher J. Evans

Designed by Corner 10 Productions

Printed in the United States of America

Second Edition

For more information, please visit:

https://www.theexpressivebook.com

The Expressive is my first book. It is the poetic expression of the many emotions I have felt from the experiences in my life broken down into three sections.

The first section is titled, "The Ways of Love." This section covers how love was discovered, hidden, developed, and shared from my early teenage years to now.

The Second section is titled, "Words Written In The Dark." This section covers my thoughts of depression, the loneliness that resulted from love being lost or never expressed, and other events in my life that have affected me in a negative way.

The final section is titled, "Experience, Reflection, and Change." This section deals with rebirth, hope, and expressing how the positive and negative events in my life have made me more understanding, appreciative, and accepting of the lessons learned from life and looking forward to what is to come.

It is my goal with *The Expressive* to not only entertain and intrigue you with my writing, but to hopefully relate to your personal experiences and emotionally connect you with the many thoughts and feelings I express in this book.

I hope you enjoy reading *The Expressive*!

Kristopher J. Evans

Contents

Section 2: Words Written In The Dark (con't.)

Section 3: Experience, Reflection, and Change

Acknowledgments

I would like to thank the people who provided me with the experiences, motivation, encouragement, love, and at times anger and disappointment, inspiring me to write *The Expressive.* This book is dedicated to you.

My Mother

My Dad

My Grandfather

My Grandmother

L.N.J.

S.H.J.

L.L.

B.C.

Stevie Wonder

The Expressive

The Ways Of Love

Real

Found my heart in her hand, my soul in her clutch,
this is strange to me because about love, I never knew much,
only gave part of me to girlfriends in the past,
if only my attention span withstood my impatience to last
long enough to for them to see the real me,
maybe then happy together we would be,
but that's then, and what's happening now is a blur,
fell deep for the first time, never thought this would occur,
I go to bed at night thinking of her with eyes dark brown,
deep enough to get lost in, often her smile lifts me when I'm down,
I frown at the negativity that surrounds me,
but it's balanced by her beauty whenever she's around me,
outstanding, not just her looks, but gifted in her mind,
anticipating intelligent conversations, plus she's so kind,
created through divine skill, with her it's like time's still,
a minute is a day, what more can I say, this feeling is real...

Two

Two souls, two hearts beating at the same time, on the same rhythm, what a wonderful melody to find.

Do I search inside me or you to understand what is true or false in my existence? One instance in my life has echoed everyday with thoughts of you as my wife...slowing my speed, in order not to move too fast. I don't want to pass this by.

I am angry with myself. "Why don't you try?" is what I ask myself while depending on a shot of Rum for help. Gradually I'm realizing my shortcomings. I feel like shedding my skin, running to the new me, but what I'm running from, first, is what I must see. As I open my eyes, I see you, so beautiful, but out of my reach. I can't physically touch you, I can only caress you with speech.

Each of us on Earth has a connection with another, whether a brother, a best friend, or a lover. I believe I'm connected to you because I think of no other. At times of despair, I imagine your smile and you are there. At times of depression, I visualize the sweet expression on your face as I stare.

You erase the negativity that nearly devoured my will, and at times, still lingers over my shoulder. The failures of my past haunt me more as I get older. You are a light whose brightness can lead me to the tunnel's end, exiting my past, and at last shedding my skin. Making me pour out that shot of Rum, filling my glass with new experiences to come, expressing myself to you, no longer forced to run away from my emotions. I envision images of the ocean, clear skies, and your eyes locked on mine. It is a feeling so intoxicating, without cares or worries about time.

I once was told that true love lasts forever, and all these years that have passed, I can honestly say I have never gone a day without you drifting on the currents flowing to my heart, bringing me to the verge of falling apart, while building me up with every new day I start.

Two souls, two hearts beating at the same time, on the same rhythm, hopefully, your heart will beat with mine.

Caves

Emotions hiding in caves, weakened it might seem,
by their existence in the dark, unexposed to sunbeams.

But in this case, they grow stronger with constant compression,
longing to be freed by the power of expression.

The sight of her face, the one they receive their power from,
is always vivid through the darkness, as they hope that one day she will come.

Although they realize that they must call to her first,
her not replying, for them would be much worse
than being tucked away in the darkness, where there is nothing but thoughts
of what could be or what could happen, and things that could not.

Is it really that they fear calling out to her, singing her name,
fearing that their voices are being projected in vain?

Or what if they fear a future where she responds with joy in her heart,

freeing them from the empty darkness, to prepare for a new start.

Maybe they are content with their conditions, living in caves,

forsaking other possibilities, to their thoughts, becoming slaves.

Gone

Music has been a love of mine, a love that has made me smile and cry,

and also remember those times when we said hello and goodbye.

It makes me think of years spent traveling down pathways I was sent

looking for ways to make you happy, at times, the wrong direction I went.

I really meant well as we fell from innocence,

my heart pains when thinking of the stains that remain from past blemishes.

Time moves swift, but it is a gift I have not unwrapped yet,

afraid to face surprises, but at the same time hoping you don't forget

the bond that was made as whispers fade into my ear,

to steer me back to the past, and at last I'm starting to hear.

Truth reveals and creates chills going up my spine,

connecting my heart, soul, and mind as if in one straight line.

What is revealed is a secret I have kept deep within,
from myself, while pondering the years you have grown closer as a friend.

With words we flirt, as with words we did hurt
but love still grew strong, much more than just a spurt.
Smiles are shared and that image is held hidden like a treasure
in my memory, when thoughts are sent to me at random, they give pleasure.

Measure the emotion that is suppressed, measure the pressure on my chest
to stand silent and be strong, is it wrong to be obsessed
on the inside if I decide to keep it there to hide?
Oppressed decisions need freedom to be expressed and not denied.

I lied to my heart and my soul felt the deception
and blocked my mind from showing my eyes a true connection.

now I'm left in a dark room where my thoughts wrestle with reality and things that could be, like could we make a happy family...a happy home?

My thoughts roam but the light in my head just came on time to bring my thoughts in and make up my mind before you're gone...

Liar

I'm a liar.
I've lied to you and myself, burying my desire.

I tried to be honest,
but fear adhered itself to my heart.

It spilled its disease
throughout my soul,
clinching my tongue,
and of my words, took control.

The thought of you in my arms
seems to harm my sensibilities,
at the same time killing me,
by not telling a simple truth.

Can I not say those words now
that I have said in the past?

At last, I can grasp the truth within
that gives me chills and makes me grin.

The words, I can shout,
now understanding what life is about.

Freedom, passion...not asking, but demanding
what was meant to be from the start...
for me to tell you I love you,
I love you with all my heart.

Passion's Light

We are both private people,
our affection shown in the shadows of passion's light.

We are motivated by random glances
with connecting stares and flirtatious smirks.

In front of watchful eyes we alter our nature
and show those in view our first kiss.

They share the moment with smiling faces,
as if it is theirs.

We don't hold back,
the wait built the pressure now released,
as the softness of your lips warms my soul
while your body is guarded by my embrace.

Our first kiss...beautiful and memorable,
now we are no longer in the shadows of passion's light,
but inside the light for the world to see the passion
that I have for you and you have for me...

The Breeze

Remembering how the breeze touched my cheek
as you now speak to me softly,
its touch combined with your voice
is so beautiful to me...

I remember how the weather
complimented my attraction to you,
warming my body, though accented
by the coolness and the calm of the breeze.

I love the playful way it tickled my neck
when we connected under the evening Sun as it set,
melting its colors into the sky,
as I revealed that smile I know you will never forget.

When my hands experienced the smoothness of your skin,
it reminded me of the breeze
that touched me when I first opened my heart to your
soul...

You are like that breeze that graced me with its presence,
attached to my memory,
but I would like to attach to your spirit
and make it one with mine.

Let the breeze return and flow against us,
speaking to our hearts in its subtle way,
so I will always remember when the breeze
first touched me that beautiful day...

Beauty Leave Slow

If you have to leave me,
then Beauty, leave me slow.

Let me know what I've known
for a little bit longer.

Love in my life is all I ask for,
but the fear of my life without it keeps me up at night
thinking about the untouched time
that could bring about change.

My smile is chipped by the sickle of unrest,
like a pest who lingers with a painful sting,
making me sing my song of light
to remain bright for the potential darkness
that manifests itself when you leave.

If you do have to leave me for good,
please Beauty, leave slow...

Open Heart

I told myself that jealousy
can not make itself a home in my heart,
but how can I not welcome it in
when you leave me with so much doubt?

You were that breeze gently tickling my brow,
but now you are a swift wind that leaves me off balance.

Your absence is an emptiness that soon fills with anger,
though I told myself anger can not live in my heart.

Deep breaths help me remember your light before it flickered
from the cold draft of my trust being stripped away.

Where are you? Why do I ask these questions and put myself through so much misery?

When one's heart is open for love, pain often sneaks in undetected and develops along side of it,
waiting to overtake what makes you smile and glow from within.

For so long, I kept my heart closed for this very reason.

Why open yourself up to heartache for moments of happiness that always appear to eventually fade?

Why smile just to inevitably touch the surrounding darkness that comes soon after disappointment?

Why?!

Because even though I am now surrounded by the darkness

with a closed heart and hollow eyes,

I remember the day I fell in love with you

and I realize all this pain is worth feeling the way I did that day...

...so eventually I will open my heart once again.

Clone

My imagination travels the same distances as when I was
a child...inventive and wild.

I imagine at times that I can just wink my eye,
and out of thin air, you would walk right by.

The dreams in my head, may be written down or said,
but what is its worth if what we had is truly dead?

To replace the irreplaceable, a feeling untraceable,
does the beauty that captured me now make me a fool?

I test the waters....can I still swim in unfamiliar tides?

Behind my search for a new beauty, an old love still hides.

I compare all to you, the stars I judged by your smile,
like I judge each new woman by your unique style.

I was blessed to know your soul, cursed to be without it,
they say there will be others, but like you, I doubt it.

I know I should move on, but for now, I fly alone,
never finding what I want, still searching for your clone.

Search

I still can see myself sharing my soul with you,
releasing control and giving into your eyes
that pulled me in whenever staring into them deeply,
traveling through love's maze.

I wish to see those days again when lost in your maze
but the exit came too fast,
what seemed like forever and could only get better
was eventually proven not to last.

I zone out at times,
my imagination gets the best of me,
it appears that swimming under the sea
or flying amongst the stars is where I should really be...

...to find what made me feel the way you made me feel.

A broken connection that has my heart left in pieces,
I'm slowly fitting the pieces where they belong
as a Stevie song is playing, I feel some peace
from the brilliant words of a master.

This particular song is not too long
so I feel depressed again soon after,
so I return,
I return to my search for that feeling.

Summer

Do you remember me?
We danced in a memory
many Summer's ago,
when I first learned about love...

When we kissed, it was like I could reach out and grab the moon,
consumed with a light
that developed from your embrace
that lovely Summer night.

The song of life I use to sing,
for you energized my spirit and would bring
joy to me by simply
looking into your eyes.

Those eyes, a path to your deepest thoughts,
a tunnel of hope,
and that smile I miss,
which on my worst days, helped me cope.

It's been years, but tears of the past
pour at times from history's reflection,
I wonder if you are traveling the world
and living your dreams, making new connections.

I ask myself aloud
as if you might be somehow listening,
when reminded of your beauty by the Sun's warm touch
or its brightness against the ocean glistening.

Do you remember me and that Summer night,
that has been embedded in my mind for so long,
or have you forgot about me over the years,
your love for me now gone?

The Expressive:

Words Written In The Dark

Like I Imagined

I never see snow where I live and although the sun shines bright, I am still cold on the inside.

Fate has told me that you will never be mine,
so I must accept the truth and move on.

I hope your new life brings you happiness. I'm not bitter, but I do still think about you.

How will I cope knowing I will never kiss you
when you wake up in the morning
or kiss you goodnight before you go to sleep?

We will never take trips to unseen lands together,
traveling the world in love like I imagined.

Rainy Mornings

On rainy mornings, I heard her voice
as the drops hit my roof and made me sad.

I wanted to smile as if this voice was real,
but the rain was all I had.

Gray skies can relate to me,
They, who also lost their vibrant view.

Pouring out their pain with force,
longing to return white and blue.

On rainy mornings, I talk to the sky,
asking, "Why did she have to go?"

The lightning strikes, showing its temper,
I guess I will never know.

Gray skies can relate to me,
we both would reverse life if we could.

Though the rain will soon pass for the sky,
but my love is gone for good.

Happiness

I've neglected myself, rejected myself,
forsaken my passions, turned my back on pleasure.

I've avoided to measure the happiness that exists,
instead I focus on the things that make me pissed.

The darkness forms and is a cloak over my soul,
a man who was once in control is now lost in a shadowed forest.

This forest of confusion that surrounds me like a maze,
leaves me in a daze, yearning for the light.

A strike to create sparks that will brighten my path,
so I can walk on an enlightened road hoping to find happiness that lasts.

My Eyes

The light in my eye dims from the shadow of life's hardships.

The anchor of wrong choices halts my progression.

My pain is visible as if my eyes are mirrors,
reflecting lost love and misplaced dreams.

Whispers from darkened corners echo in my mind,
as my heart soaks in the faint words,
reminding me of my failures in the past
that form a tower of doubt.

Why do my eyes lose focus when opportunity approaches,
suffering the sharpness of Fear's blade by my own hand?

Cut by cut, each slice causes my eyes to widen,
revealing the brightness of hope that still exist,
leaving fear with no place to hide in
but I feel the tightness of my eyelids returning.

Fear has won yet again,
as the burning from the brightness becomes too much,
enemy and friend, both living within,
who limit what I can touch.

My reach is stunted, what I wanted to be
is not just out of reach,
but now even too far away for my eyes to see...
a lesson learned, but not one I can ever teach.

The Dark, Deep Sea

I feel like I was born not to care,
I stare off into space often questioning myself.

When I do emerge from the depths of the dark sea of solitude,
I quickly return to the deep where I wish I could just sleep.

Instead, I'm haunted by my thoughts and suffer from late nights with restless visions,
focused on the ceiling fan turning and reminding me of hours lost each night.

My soul fights with my heart, a better man wants to emerge,
but the urge to remain the same wins and ends the internal struggle.

I juggle my emotions, closing out those close to me,
treating them like they are supposed to see the true me without me revealing it.

I want them to see what I can be,
I need to emerge once more from the depths of the sea.

I decided to show my love to those I feel have earned it,
I did this recently, and this love, they never returned it.
My passion was broken, so my love, I burned it,
and the dark, deep sea was home to me once again.

Walls

I find comfort with the walls,
their silence absorbing my joy and pain.

A subtle transfer of thoughts and emotions,
my protection from judgmental voices.

A choice to keep others from entering my space,
no reason for me to face anyone but myself,
surrounded by many, confronted by none,
I am but one inside an invisible sphere.

That sphere is inside a box with no windows or door,
all I want to explore is before me in plain view to see.

Constantly, fists are pounding
as the reverberated effect becomes drowned out
by the rebellious nature my will has developed,
soon pounding fists morph into shouts.

My name they yell, with lead hearts, they fail,
also drowned out as the walls grow more dense.

Outsiders see it as a hell or a self-developed cell,
but from the outside, what can they really tell?

Mortal

People gathered around my body,
no need for an autopsy,
simply I got shot three
times in the chest, as I begin to rest
on the street, taken off my feet,
eyes crying, soon I'll be dying,
thinking of my days in the future,
erased by my shooter.

Mental calamity, to handle these
emotions taking place now,
inside of me, it's like a riot three
times worst than you could imagine.

Although, in a way I'm laughing,
leaving this world ain't all bad
I've had some sad days,
life is a maze, I'm 'bout to get out
and see a new world,
and what waits for me as I watch the unknown unfurl,
the equilibrium,
my mind is caught between two worlds.

Will my soul release,
so I can have peace?
I feel like my heart is stopping...
am I now deceased?

Mind

I got lost in a fantasy, discovered a new reality,
walking the halls of my mind, exploring my mentality.

Some corridors were dark, but lightened as I moved on,
Seeing sights I've never seen, while hearing an unfamiliar song.

It echoed through my thoughts, becoming more familiar with time,
I encountered many people speaking in codes, offering signs.

Signs of things that could be and things I'd never see,
Then I realized these people were all different versions of me.

They each gave me insight and advice for my daily living,
such as forgiving others and to become more giving.

Then all at once they surrounded me and began to change form,
the inside of my head became as turbulent as a storm.

All my identities turned into shadows, and grew smirks of pure deceit,

I quickly recognized these new forms as the sides of me I did not want to meet.

They spoke of dark things, opposite of what I was first told,

instructing me to care for only myself from now to the day I am old.

When questions began to surface to ask these dark manifestations,

they slowly faded away, then I felt a strange sensation.

My head quickly felt light and soon my legs became unstable,

I passed out and then awoke flat on a hospital table.

The doctor said I died, but was brought back in no time,

so maybe I walked in a place much more mysterious than my mind.

Comfortable

My smile shows when the darkness leaves,
but it hovers over me usually, so I am rarely happy.

Forcing joy is a broken toy that I continue to play with,
knowing that no satisfaction will come from it.

Yet, I continue trying to alter my mood that naturally exists,
just to eventually return to my corner of solitude where I feel most comfortable.

I must make myself uncomfortable,
that is the way of breaking the destructive cycle I peddle.

I'm sick of this repetition of doubt, stress, and solitude.
No longer will I settle!

The Expressive:

Experience, Reflection, and Change

Time

I waited too long it seems,
Seems like time is losing its patience,
Patience is something I think I need more,
More time though is what I crave.

My youth is telling me to move faster,
Faster, time runs the race of life,
Life is too short to not fulfill my dreams,
Dreams I have are only blocked by the grave.

Age will show you how to live,
Live everyday with passion and hope,
Hope for only positive results,
Results, in time, will be an open mind.

Pursue your dreams and don't follow others,
Others have their own path to take,
Take your time and learn yourself,
Yourself, you will eventually find.

Rebirth of Thought

I keep walking down the wrong path in my search for Ms. Right,

my mind is corrupted from past flights that ended in non-fatal crashes,

although wreckage and ashes cling to my heart,

still I will keep looking to meet a mate for my soul.

Looking while asking unanswered questions in a riddle called Life,

where blind dates help me see

that my time is worth more than

supplying a free dinner, movie, and a hug.

I feel like I'm losing control,

I look at my friends starting their families,

outside, I'm happy to still be a bachelor,

if you could see the inside, you would see the impatience building to a higher degree.

when is it my turn to learn fatherhood?

I want to stop a child's cries with the sound of my voice,

I guess it has been my choice

at least that's what my ex told me.

We are still in contact and we speak of such things,
on how wedding rings could have been in the future
but hope brings disappointment at times
and regret is an enemy I avoid.

So I decided to stop worrying and hurrying the future,
and let life take its course,
until I meet the one who will give birth to my daughter or son,
becoming a union of one.

I will no longer run after fate but take each day at a time
developing my dreams and creating with dedication,
I will cut off those that use me
and fake friends who never really knew me.

I will make new friends and discover new places,
learn the history of other races and cultures,
energize under the rays of the sun,
and have fun seeing the world for it's beauty.

Growth

Enriched in thought which brought me
to staircases of infinite scale,
stories to tell dwell behind unforseen walls
producing voices that call out my name.

Strange to my ears,
although the same words echo with appeal.

A tunnel with footprints that lead into darkness,
a torch in hand to light my path,
visions of a novice who will develop in his office,
and illustrate the art of growth and passion.

Outlasting fear,
the shaking hands that use to steer,
now grip the wheel with confidence,
because that is all I feel.

New days ahead, where when I stare
to analyze my surroundings,
I see sunshine instead of cloudy displays,
with each new day I experience what being proud brings.

I had to open my eyes
to witness what I was meant to see,
before I coud begin my growth,
and become what I am meant to be.

Clear Vision

I live my life with clear vision,
fear missing my soul,
I hold knowledge,
that stays polished to abolish the mold,
and mental mildew, while some still do
hold on to ignorance,
and the little sense that they have
stays masked and hidden in
the darkest part of the brain,
but I maintain to be on the go,
so I can elevate minds
to find what is needed to grow,
conversations with older generations,
taking notes with patience,
learned information will be erased
when empty dreams are chased and
never caught, I was taught
that life will go on without you,
so I feel the way to keep up
is constantly trying to outdo
my past achievements,
self-esteem is the first thing that's needed,

because even followers can rise up
in a group and lead it,
if you have a vision, clearly see it,
then in your grasp, it can be
with hard work and dedication,
positive results you will see,
remember that wisdom comes from knowledge,
so knowledge you must find,
to find knowledge,
you must develop your mind.

Stevie

I was listening to Stevie Wonder
while writing these words,
astonished by his vision of life
only through what he has heard.

To be blind does not mean
that you can not see,
for the images we project
from our minds can actually be
the reality that our eyes
can't witness without believing
that anything is possible,
and knowing that doubters are deceiving.

I want to be like a King,
but first, in my heart it should be known,
a king sitting on a throne
needs no confirmation from others of what he owns.

Mediocre ways or superior actions,
How will you choose to live?
Will you only take with a clutched heart
or be full of love, willing to give?

My goal in life is have a goal,
you might ask what do I mean,
Basically I want to keep going,
forever chasing new dreams.

Stevie helped me choose superior actions,
simply from the beauty of his music,
if I can just reflect a small amount of that beauty,
then to the world I will never be useless.

Mediocre ways or superior actions,
the choice is yours to decide,
I decided to embrace my dreams and live them fully,
win or fail, no one can say I never tried.

Stepping Stones

I was told by my Mom about stepping stones,
in life we encounter many kind...
our friends, enemies, lovers, and our jobs,
they all come to mind.

A stepping stone is something that prepares you for greater things to come,
I can see the value in many, but have not yet recognized it in some.
Relationships seem so strong, although many wither away like a rose
that is long past its day, they say "that's life", I suppose...

Even when friendships fade with time and your heart you gave is returned,
life still goes on, as do you, and many lessons are learned.
Those lessons are blessings from God that will help you as you age,
the story of the life we live has more than just one page.

I've encounter many stepping stones and I have grown wiser, I hope...
I've learned to expect the unexpected and I have learned how to cope.

I know how to bounce back from anything that might seem to break me down,

I know how to smile brightly when others think I should carry a frown.

Please try to grow from every experience, because this is what I plan to do,

if we ever crossed paths in the past, I hope I was a stepping stone for you.

New Road

A tear from my eye, down my cheek, what is this feeling?
Until I got older, I didn't know it was God's healing.

Allowing me to release my frustrations, because on occasion,
I look pain in the face, in a place deep where I can taste
the agony of demons attacking me, I know it sounds like I'm insane,
sometimes I think I have to be to maintain.

Born a healthy baby, cloaked in sin, with the gift of redemption,
I asked the doctor in the sky for a prescription.

Generously he gave, no longer am I a slave
to the ways of the wicked, now a new road has been paved.

Your Words Are Heard

I know sometimes the world can be
like a barb-wired cage around your peace.

I know those closest to us at times
deliver to us the most pain.

You might question the Father
as to if He is even listening,
believing your words are unheard in the sky,
descending to once again rejoin your heartache.

That is understandable, but the truth is
your words are heard!

It is just that you compare your time to His,
that is the problem.

His time is perfect,
regardless if it is not on your schedule.

The peace you seek will be offered,
but sometimes we need unrest in our lives to help find the best within us.

A storm rages, bright skies dim, and thunder will rumble,
but sunshine spreads the clouds, eventually bringing light back to conquer the dark.

The light I recognize within you will soon explode
for the world to see,
and instead of a cage, the world will be open for you to explore,
and show who you are and will soon be.

Dream Visit

I feel like I need to pay a visit
to my Grandpa's grave site,
I think to those days
when we used to hang tight
back in the 80's
when my cousin and I stayed nights
and days at his place,
Fabian, you remember those days, right?

He came to see me in a dream
about a year ago.
He spoke to tell me although he's gone,
he's still with me, ya know?

I woke up that night crying
because I knew it was real,
we sat down in his old house
and he asked me how I feel.

I replied, I'm doing good
but I wish that you could
have seen me graduate from high school
and survive the hood,

I wish you could have seen me in college
and earn two degrees.
I wish you could - he cut me off and said:
grandson please...

I was there when you walked the stage,
receiving those degrees,
I've been by your side through your struggles,
this, grandson, please believe.

I'm here right now in this dream,
call it a favor from God,
with Him all is possible,
although to you this seems odd.

I'm checking in on you to let you know
that I am proud,
I know you're still sad,
but you know about dark clouds...

They have silver linings,
just reminding you the Sun will shine,
I'm not here in the physical
but you are still on my mind.

Grandson, you have grown
to be a nice young man
and when your heart is troubled,
in spirit, by you I stand.

It's time for me to go, Kris,
I'm so glad that I could meet
you at the age you are now,
goodbye until the next time we speak.

Flight

As I rocketed toward the sky,
I saw the stars in amazement,
shooting past me as I flew
at a speed that seemed untrue.

I slowed down to drift past
planets known to me and planets unknown.
I spoke with different cultures and races
in strange languages and in new places.

I shook hands with distant beings
with strange smiles and spectacular eyes,
as my journey led me to a planet of light,
so bright, the sky appeared to be pure white.

I soon found my view was my bedroom
after awaking from these thoughts of travel,
thinking that I prefer my dreams of flight
to a life cemented to the ground night after night.

Italy

Now this is the kind of beauty to share with the one you love,

a new view that connects to my heart and nourishes my soul,

this is the place that will stay with me forever,

I am a new man after this experience,

a savage mind can be refined by such sights,

ignorance enlightened infinitely,

a weakened spirit strengthened to its limit,

art so historic from a culture with a deep past,

the passion that created it brings out my passion equally,

I long to create, build, and write with the greatness of what I see before me,

this language, when spoken, attracts me with the simplest of words,

women here can smile and it will take your breath away,

arguably the best food on the planet,

sadness on the day I must return home but happiness for what I have been a part of,

my love is here and a piece of this place will come back with me,

Thank you, Italy...Grazie, Italia.

Lost Time

Lost time, yeah...Where did the time go?

I want to say things haven't changed
but they definitely have.

Gone are the care-free nights
when we laughed until we passed out,
reminiscing on the hours before
and planning to do the exact thing the next night.

The young eyes I once saw in the mirror
look less vibrant now
and my laugh is a bit raspier
than in those days.

My heart continues to be strong with passion
but still there is something missing,
maybe because the many memories that have holes I long to fill,
resurrect those times that are now impossible to find.

I am amazed at how life can be such a blur,
wondering where did the days go? Yeah, lost time...

Tomorrow

Where will I be tomorrow?
Will sorrow try to be my friend again?
Am I going to stay quiet like yesterday
and keep all my thoughts within?

Is life slowly breaking me down,
so one day I'll reform to be complete?
Will I lose a friend that I considered loyal
or suffer a love one's deceit?

What will I do tomorrow,
live in the past or move ahead?
Am I going to contradict myself
or back up what I said?

Who will I meet tomorrow,
an unknown enemy or future wife?
Will I learn anything I don't know today
that will better me for the rest of my life?

New Light

Driving with one eye on the road and the other eye to a dream,
half awake in a city that screams my name.
I block out the rage that makes people around me
act like animals in a cage.

I still find myself somewhat connected,
while looking for something to fully sever the link.
Burned out with repetition, is there a petition
I can sign for peace of mind.

I focus on those same old lights that tell me my next move,
contemplating how to escape this groove that is off key.
Searching for that melody that compliments my life,
and answers those questions that poke my heart like a dull knife.

What is it I need to find the key to the door to explore the destiny touched in dreams while in rest?

What test must I pass to at last see the best in me
revealing the truth for both my eyes to see?

The day flows, not like a gentle stream,
but a leaking faucet with a mildewed spout.
I withdraw from my surroundings, hoping for time to fast
forward, or rewind to days when I had less doubt.

I can not go backwards so I must live right now,
as each second takes more away from my existence.
Persistence and efforts must be made to shine new light
on the shade that has compromised the early path that was
laid.

Let me walk with confidence, a common prayer
there in my heart as I greet the morning light of the sun.
I don't want to run from the strength within to form a
weakened spirit,
I know Fear is a villain that plots against me for fun.

Instead, I will stomp the path laid with a determined mind
and strong spirit,
sparking my own light to direct my next move towards
the new.

The future is what I make it, time to take it and claim it
for myself,
waiting for the new light, no more old lights telling me
what to do.

Tell Me, Help Me, Guide Me, Love Me

One night in a prayer, I asked God
to tell me what to do, help me to do it, and guide me as I do it...

Tell my heart not to ache, tell my mind what to find,
tell my feet where to go, tell my soul things divine.

Help me grow to be great, help me see the unseen,
help me touch the world, help me say what I mean.

Guide me through the dark, guide me though the light,
guide me to peace within, guide me when I fight.

I realized that I ask for so much when He asks me for so little,
and all he wants from me is simple and easy to do.

He responds to my requests...

Love me with all you have,
love me so true,
love me unconditionally,
love me as I love you...

About the Author

Kristopher J. Evans was born and raised in Bakersfield, CA. Although he went to art school to study graphic design and computer animation, he has been writing since he was in the first grade. Having a mother who writes poetry and short stories as a hobby, and is also a local playwright, the love of writing rubbed off on him at an early age.

The Expressive is Kristopher's first book of poetry. He is already in the process of developing more poetry books.

When not writing, Kristopher is running his home based business, Corner 10 Productions, that specializes in graphic design, website development, event photography and photo booth services. You can learn more about Corner 10 Productions at https://www.corner10.com.

www.ingramcontent.com/pod-product-compliance
Ingram Content Group UK Ltd.
Pitfield, Milton Keynes, MK11 3LW, UK
UKHW041920190726
13854UKWH00003B/1357

9 781387 624232